The Names of Leesburg

Historic Origins of the Names of the Town's Streets, Parks, Homes and More

By

Bob Regan

Photos by

Jeff Wingard

The Names of Leesburg: Historic Origins of the Towns Streets, Parks, Homes, and More
Copyright © 2009 by Bob Regan
Photography by Jeff Wingard

ISBN-13: 978-0-615-32823-2
ISBN-10: 0615328237

Cover photo: "Central View in Leesburg" detail, from Yardley Taylor: Map of Loudoun County, Virginia from Actual Surveys. 1 inch = 1 mile. Philadelphia: Thomas Reynolds & Robert Pearsall Smith, Publishers. Map Collection, Thomas Balch Library, Leesburg, VA.

| Dedication

This brief tome is formally dedicated to Ms. Vinton Liddell Pickens whose tireless pioneering and determined efforts in the area of land planning and zoning saved Leesburg, and indeed much of Loudoun County, from unregulated urban sprawl. Without her work Leesburg would not be the Leesburg it is today.

Also, as usual, this work is informally dedicated to two Leesburg natives, my grandsons Zack and Brian.

| Contents

Dedication...iii

Preface..1

Introduction..3

The Town...5

    Flag...9

    Some Historical Highlights..................................10

        Railroad..10

        Ferries and Turnpikes.................................11

        Civil War Forts...13

        Leesburg's Capitol Connections..............15

        Airport...17

    Notable Residents...18

    Names of Some Nearby Features........................19

Buildings, Homes, and Schools...............................21

    Buildings...22

    Water Tanks..34

    Homes...35

    Schools...41

Streets...45

    Leesburg Street Names......................................46

        General...47

        Some Specific Street Names......................50

Parks and Subdivisions...55

    Parks...56

    Subdivisions...62

Afterword..67

References...69

Author and Photographer..71

Index..73

Photo Gallery...77

| Preface

"The name we give something,
shapes our attitude to it."
–Katherine Patterson

This work evolved out of several visits to my grandchildren who live in Leesburg. While residing in a relatively new home, they are located comfortably close to the historic downtown area and many visits included walks to downtown, usually with accompanying wagons, tricycles, bicycles, etc.

I was often struck by the fact that the new blended so comfortably with the old in this area and repeatedly marveled at how Leesburg had retained its historic identity (and dignity) while also steadily growing and adapting to meet the needs of the twentieth century.

I have written several local history books on the place of my residence, Pittsburgh, and decided to do one on Leesburg. There have been many wonderful books written on Leesburg. This is both remarkable, when you consider the size of the town, and also a tribute to the long historic lineage of the town. I certainly have no intention on intruding on these works. However what does strike me is that much of the town's history is preserved and presented in the names given to the streets, buildings and subdivisions. These are used routinely throughout every day but little attention is paid to the meaning behind them. Thus, this work evolved which is a study of the names that adorn the town of Leesburg.

This then is the story primarily of the origin of the names of many of the town's features as well as the origin and development of many of the features themselves. It is offered in the hope that it may help residents and visitors to further enjoy and appreciate Leesburg.

Bob Regan, September 2009

| Introduction

"Local names...are never mere arbitrary sounds,
devoid of meaning. They may always be regarded
as records of the past, inviting and rewarding
a careful historical interpretation"
–Isaac Taylor, *Words and Places*

Leesburg is a captivating town. Indeed it could, and should, be used as an example of well controlled suburban development. Close scrutiny of the entire town reveals a well preserved historic downtown area surrounded by well controlled and planned twentieth century commercial and residential developments that do not diminish the appeal of the entire town. In Leesburg you have a town that while still serving as the center of government and commerce for Loudoun County evokes a feeling of an era long ago. Indeed the downtown historic district is an authentic town center and routinely cited as one of the best-preserved and most picturesque downtowns in the state. Yet, within easy walking distance are modern homes in comfortable settings as well as current commercial establishments.

All of the new and some of the old streets, buildings, and subdivisions are of necessity adorned with names. And the names given to a town's various entities such as these typically reflect various aspects of its nature, culture, and history. Knowing the stories behind such names can help one to better understand and appreciate the locale.

The many proper and familial names used throughout Leesburg are thus one more element that adds to its overall charm. However in addition to using the names in one's daily life, it is also worthwhile and interesting (I hope) to discover their origin.

In any study such as this it is important to clarify the terms of the study and the first step is to consider a dictionary definition of the word *name*. One of the most succinct is that a name is a label for a thing, person, place, product (as in a brand name), and even an idea or concept, normally used to distinguish one from another. In the search for that definition I discovered that there is an American Name Society (True!). It was founded in 1951 to promote onomastics, the study of names and naming practices, both in the United States and abroad. It seeks to find out what really is in a name, and to investigate cultural insights, settlement history, and linguistic characteristics revealed in names. A branch of onomastics is toponymy, which is the study of toponyms or place names. So, welcome to a toponymic study of Leesburg.

| The Town

"Leesburg! Paradise of the youthful warrior!
Land of excellent edibles and beautiful maidens!"
–Confederate artilleryman in late 1861

Being the first town in the county, Leesburg and Loudoun County are intimately connected as both share a fairly common heritage and history. However, the Town of Leesburg veritably exudes history. Its picturesque quaintness masks the fact that it was the home of a U.S. President, once the repository of the Declaration of Independence and the Constitution, the source of the building material for the U.S. Capitol, and the place where the Monroe Doctrine was written.

Thus it is worthwhile in addition to exploring the development of the names of the County and Town to highlight a little of Leesburg's colorful past. This by no means is a complete account and those intrigued by some of these facts are urged to seek out some of the references cited at the end of this work for more complete information.

In many of the original states, the counties that were initially established covered broad geographic areas as the population was typically scattered throughout the region. However, as the population grew, particularly in areas far from the county seat, necessitating long and arduous journeys to the county courthouse, there often was a move to form a new county. This is the manner in which Loudoun County came to be.

The "back country inhabitants" (how future Loudouners were referred to in their petition to form a county), because of the great hardships they were under by being so far away from the present seat of justice and public offices, petitioned for the creation of a new county. Loudoun County was thus formed when it separated from Fairfax County. Specifically, in 1757, by act of the Virginia House of Burgesses, Fairfax County was divided. The western portion was named Loudoun for John Campbell, Fourth Earl of Loudoun (1705-1782), a Scottish nobleman who served as Commander-in-Chief for all British armed forces in North America and was titular Governor of Virginia from 1756 to 1768. The eastern boundary has varied a little over the years as the original eastern boundary was formed by Difficult Run and Little Rocky Run, ten miles east of the present boundary which was set in 1798.

There undoubtedly was a settlement or outpost of some sort at the locale of Leesburg long before its official recorded history. This is due to the fact that Leesburg was located at the intersection of major east-west and north-south roads that probably evolved from Indian foot/horse paths.

It is known that in the 1750s a small settlement existed here at the crossroads of the Carolina and Alexandria Roads. The Carolina Road was the north-south road going from Frederick, Maryland to the Carolinas. It basically ran along today's King Street. The east-west road, along Loudoun Street, was known as the Alexandria Road but was also referred to as the Great Road, Vestal's Gap Road, Shenandoah Road, and Potomac Ridge Road. John Carlyle owned the land and leased it to the county's first land developer, Nicholas Minor. Minor established a tavern at the intersection.

Upon the formation of Loudoun County (April, 1757) Minor purchased the leased land plus additional acreage from Carlyle. Although there were scant few buildings besides his tavern, Minor named the area Georgetown, in honor of the then King of England George II.

Leesburg is located approximately in the center of Loudoun County and it had some establishments. Accordingly, on June 15, 1758, the British Colonial Council ordered the establishment of a courthouse at the crossroads, effectively making Georgetown the county seat. Seizing upon this opportunity, Minor had John Hough survey a town of sixty acres which contained six cross streets and sixty half-acre lots. The streets were named King, Church, Back, Royal, Loudoun and Market. Minor was quite serious about developing the town as he required people who purchased lots to build

East Market and Fayette Streets: Historic postcards, 1900-2008 (VC 0004). Thomas Balch Library, Leesburg, VA.

substantial (for the time) dwellings. Today, any extant house from that time is known as a covenant house.

Minor's gamble paid off as that fall (October 12, 1758) the Virginia General Assembly established the town of Leesburg on the 60 acres that Minor had lain out. The town was named for Thomas Lee, an influential land speculator and one time acting governor of Virginia who died in office in 1750. It is a fitting name for this locale as the name Lee developed in England from Leaz or Leah meaning "wood clearing" or "plain or untitled land."

Fifty-five years later on February 13, 1813 Leesburg was incorporated as a town and became the first incorporated town in Loudoun County. John Rose was selected as the first mayor.

It is interesting to note, especially for a Pittsburgher, that when the Leesburg post office was established in 1803, it was named Leesburgh. Throughout the United States all municipalities ending in –burg either used –burg or –burgh or sometimes both. To settle the matter of whether to "h" a burg (burgh) or not the United States Board of Geographic Names decided in 1890 that the standard would be –burg. This did not settle well with Pittsburghers who had been using –burgh since the establishment of that City in 1816. Following a steady and massive protest from the residents of that city the Board decided in 1911 that Pittsburgh (and only Pittsburgh) could use the final h. Thus, Pittsburgh is the only burg in the United States that is a burgh and Leesburgh became, once again, Leesburg.

Flag

On September 14, 2008, The Town of Leesburg celebrated its 250th birthday. During that celebration, the city unveiled its new flag. This flag resembles the center part of the Lee family coat of arms that was in use by the Lee Family of Virginia when Leesburg was founded in 1758. The blue and yellow checkerboard band on the red background represents the Lee Family Coat of Arms and the white Cinquefoil (five petal flower) on a blue background comes from the Astley Family Coat of Arms. The coats of arms were quartered with the white cross indicating Leesburg as a crossroads.

The Lee family is descendant from one of the oldest families in England and in the fourteenth century their fortune and estates were merged with the Astley family through the marriage of a Robert Lee with Margaret Astley in 1385. Since that time the Lee family coat of arms has included the five petal flower of the Astlety coat of arms. The Astleys derived their name from the Manor of Astley and the name was originally Eastley meaning "east leigh" or "east wood."

Some Historical Highlights

As previously noted, Leesburg abounds in history, especially as it was involved in the French and Indian War, the War of 1812, and the Civil War. This section, while not addressing all of the town's history, highlights some elements of the areas colorful past.

Railroad

In 1860 The Alexandria, Loudoun and Hampshire Railroad (later to be known as the Washington & Old Dominion Railroad or W&OD) reached Leesburg. This short-line railroad eventually was extended to Bluemont at the foot of the Blue Ridge Mountains near Snickers Gap, not far from the boundary line between Virginia and West Virginia. The railroad started operation in 1847, passenger service (it was also known as the Virginia Creeper) ceased in 1951, and freight service and the railroad in 1968.

Railroad Depot: Historic postcards, 1900-2008 (VC 0004). Thomas Balch Library, Leesburg, VA.

Ferries and Turnpikes

Little River Turnpike was the first major turnpike in the United States. A General Assembly Act of 1809 called for the construction of the Leesburg Turnpike (Rte. 7) to connect Leesburg to the Little River Turnpike. At the beginning of the Civil War, the road was abandoned as a toll road. Broad Run Bridge and Toll House at the intersection of Route 28 and Route 7 are the only remnants of this turnpike. The prevalence of turnpikes is attested by the fact that in 1875 there were four tollhouses in Leesburg. One for the Leesburg Turnpike, one for the Point of Rocks Turnpike, one for the Aldie Turnpike, and one for Snickersville Turnpike.

By 1806 there were six or seven ferries crossing the Potomac to serve Loudoun County. Some of these were:

Edwards Ferry—operated by Benjamin Edwards.

Claphams Ferry—This ferry was started by Josias Clapham, a Revolutionary War hero, in 1757. It was later owned and operated by John Spinks and known as Spinks ferry.

Aubrey's Ferry—started in 1741 by Francis Aubrey near Point of Rocks, this was the first of the ferries to traverse the Potomac River. This may also be spelled Awbrey.

Nolands Ferry—Operated by Philip Noland.

Payne's Ferry—little information is available on this ferry but it appears that it was connected with Flayl Payne and was sometimes called Frail Pain's Ferry.

White's ferry was not one of these as it didn't start operation until 1828 and before that time people, especially Civil War troops, crossed near the location of the ferry in a shallow area known as White's ford. The ferry was originally known as

*White's Ferry (top and center) and its guidance cable reel
(left).*

Conrad's Ferry. However, following the Civil War, Loudoun
resident and Confederate hero (of the Laurel Brigade) Elijah
Viers White purchased the operation. The ferryboat "Jubal A.
Early" is named for the confederate officer who crossed the
river here after his raid on Washington DC in 1864.

It is interesting to note that near the Maryland terminus of the
ferries was a canal developed by Patowmack Company Canal
(predecessor of C&O) which was the first man made waterway
in the U.S.

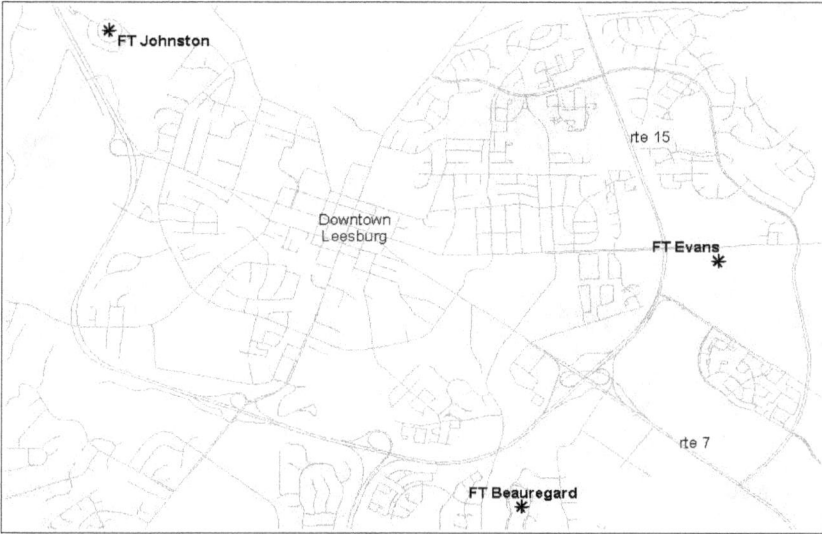

Locations of Civil War forts in Leesburg.

Civil War Forts

Leesburg was a staging ground for the British during the French and Indian War and for the Colonials during the Revolutionary War. During the Civil War, Leesburg was a strategic point for troop movements.

In 1861 at least three earthen forts were built to protect Leesburg from possible invasion after Virginia seceded from the Union. These were Forts Beauregard, Johnston, and Evans. Although Fort Beauregard has been completely lost the other two remain.

Fort Evans—named for General Nathan George "Shank" Evans: The fort was built in 1861 along Edwards Ferry Road to protect the approaches to the town from the Potomac River. From the fort, General Evans successfully orchestrated the defense of Leesburg during the Battle of Ball's Bluff, which was the largest battle to occur during the Civil War in Loudoun

Aerial View of Fort Evans. Image from U.S. Geological Survey.

County. Largely intact today, the fort is roughly rectangular as viewed from above, about 100 yards across, with artillery bastions at the corners. It is bounded by earthen walls 5 feet high and 30 feet thick.

The fort is located on land that once housed the Carr family estate and now is the site of the North American headquarters of Rehau, a Switzerland-based plastic company. Interestingly, the fort is located only a few hundred feet from the Home Depot store on Fort Evans Road.

Fort Beuregard, which was long ago obliterated, was located southeast of town on a high point in what is now the Beuregard Estates subdivision. Its location was very near today's Fortress Circle.

A picnic table sits just outside Fort Evans at it appears today.

Fort Johnston was a star shaped fort built on the highest point near Leesburg just northwest of town off present day Route 7. Remnants of the fort still exist but are located on private property on, naturally, Ft. Johnston Road.

Leesburg's Capitol Connections

In 1814 during the war of 1812, Leesburg served as a temporary haven for the US government and its archives including the Declaration of Independence, the Articles of Confederation, the Constitution, much of George Washington's correspondences, and Congressional and State Department records. Twenty-two wagonloads of documents were brought and stored first at Philip Nolands House (now known as Constitution House and located at 11 Cornwall Street) and then at Rokeby, on Gleedsdale Road south of the town, where there

Constitution House (Philip Noland's House).

was more adequate and secure storage space. They remained there for several weeks.

Stone from Leesburg was used to build and rebuild the U .S. Capitol. The source was two quarries at the south end of Leesburg (one still exists—Luck Stone Quarry). Potomac marble is not really marble but a limestone conglomerate, i.e., a mixture of limestone imbedded with pebbles. When polished it looks like marble. Thus the Capitol is built of faux marble from Leesburg. Real marble from Vermont would have been impractical, at that time, to transport to the capitol site. More recently, rocks from this quarry have been used to simulate the lunar surface in some scientific studies.

Leesburg Executive Airport at Godfrey Field.

Airport

Leesburg's original airport was owned by radio and television personality Arthur Godfrey and was located off Edwards Ferry Road between Catoctin Circle and Plaza Street. Godfrey was an avid aviator and used his own DC-3 to commute weekly to New York to do his radio and television shows. The noise of his DC-3 ultimately became a nuisance as the Town developed, so in the early 1960s Godfrey sold the field and donated a portion of the profits to the town for the construction of a new airport two miles south of town. The new aiport, built in 1963, was originally named Godfrey Field but the name was eventually changed to the Leesburg Executive Airport at Godfrey Field. The new airport terminal was named in honor of Stanley F. Caulkins, a long time Leesburg resident, staunch advocate of the airport, and once chairman of the Airport Authority.

Notable Residents

George C. Marshall—General George C. Marshall (1880-1959) was author of the Marshal Plan and lived at Dodona Manor on Edwards Ferry Road from 1941 to 1959. Marshall was Leesburg's most famous resident, but some other notable Leesburg locals are listed below.

James Dickey—While James Dickey was the poetry consultant to the Library of Congress he lived in Leesburg at the Glenfiddich house on North King Street. During 1966 to 1968 while residing here he wrote the first draft of his 1970 novel entitled "Deliverance."

Arthur Godfrey—Arthur Godfrey (1903-1983) rivaled Marshall as Leesburg's most notable resident. During the 1950s he was perhaps televisions most prolific personality hosting two weekly shows as well as a daily show. A skilled pilot he was responsible for the establishment of the Leesburg airport. Godfrey lived at his home, Beacon Hill, a 1,970 acre estate (now a housing development) just west of Leesburg. He is buried in Union Cemetery.

Lyndon LaRouche—The infamous political activist, and founder of several political organizations in the United States and elsewhere, known collectively as the LaRouche movement lived amid many armed guards for several years at the Woodburn estate.

Colonel John Mosby—He led the 43rd Batallion Partisan Rangers, known as Mosby and his Raiders. The mascot of Loudoun County High School (The Raiders) is named for this group as is the Mosbby Heritage Area located in Atoka which spans five counties.

Rudolph Nureyev—famed ballet dancer once owned and lived at Woodburn, just south of the town.

Names of Some Nearby Features

Aldie—Settled by Charles Fenton Mercer and named by him for Aldie Castle, his ancestral home in Scotland.

Alogonkian—A large group of Indian tribes in North America.

Balls Bluff—The bluff was named after the Ball family, which owned the riverfront farm at the time. They were related to George Washington's mother, Mary Ball Washington.

Goose Creek—The Algonquin name (Cokongoloto) for this creek meant "River of Geese" as they prized feathers, thus the name. There once (1854) was a Goose Creek Canal from Evergreen Mills to the Potomac.

Lucketts—Known as Goresville after the name of prominent local landowner, Thomas Gore. The name was finally changed to Lucketts in 1865, named for Thomas Hussey Luckett, son-in-law of ferry owner and property speculator Philip Noland.

Paeonian Springs—Named from the Greek word meaning "health giving."

Sterling—Originally named Buchanan after President James Buchanan who lived there.

Sycolin—An intriguing name, undoubtedly named for the Sycolin Tribe, which was an offshoot of the Tuscarora Indians. However there is no known translation of the word Sycolin. The name once had an *e* at the end when a post office was there from 1885-1905.

| Buildings, Homes, and Schools

The word building dates back to 1297 and derives from Old English byldan to construct a house.

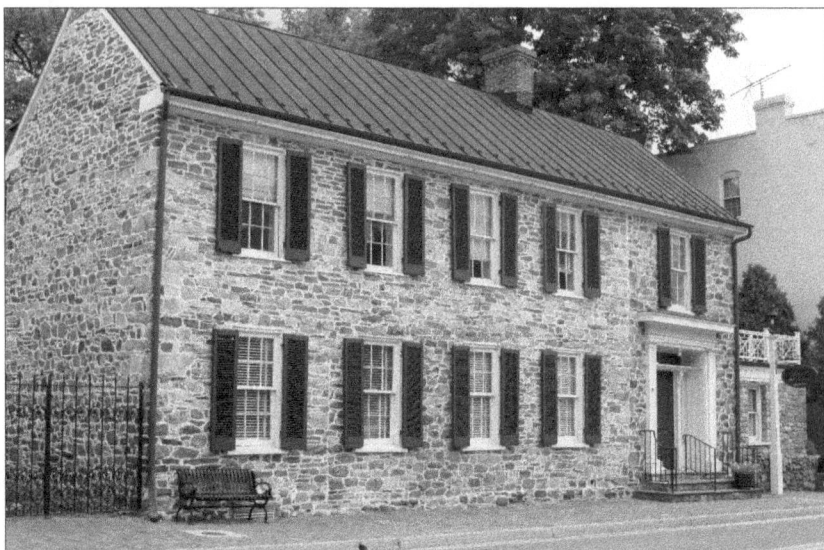

Laurel Brigade Inn.

Buildings

<u>Immaculate Conception Church</u>

The little white church as 231 North King Street, built in 1878, is now known as the Chapel of the Immaculate Conception and part of the nearby St John the Apostle church.

<u>Laurel Brigade Inn</u>

In 1946 the building that had served as a hotel and private residence once again became an Inn and was named in honor of the Civil War Brigade, led by a local confederate, Col. Elijah V. White (after whom White's ferry is named).

Immaculate Conception Church.

Lightfoot Restaurant.

Lightfoot Restaurant

Built in 1888, this building operated as The People's National Bank for over 50 years. It was restored in 1999 and became a fine dining restaurant. Lightfoot Restaurant was named to honor Francis Lightfoot Lee, son of Thomas Lee. Francis Lightfoot Lee lived in Loudoun County, signed the Declaration of Independence, and brought up the bill to establish Leesburg.

Leesburg Academy Building
The Leesburg Academy, a classical school for boys was founded in 1797 and the latest building was constructed in 1848. According to former Leesburg Mayor and County Supervisor Frank Raflo, the building has a Temple form of Roman Ionic portico, unlike most porticoes in Virginia, which are Greek Revival. On July 15, 1873, the Loudoun County Board of Supervisors received a proposal from a committee of the Academy's Board of Trustees and voted to purchase the

Old Loudoun County Courthouse.

Loudoun County Courthouse.

building, which was next to the Courthouse, to house the Clerks office.

The matching building to the east was constructed in 1959. Both buildings were part of two court expansion projects, first in the late 1970s, and again in 2000-2001.

Leesburg Constitution house

Philip Nolands House at 11 Cornwal Street is referred to as The Constitution House, as the Constitution and other government documents were first briefly stored here before being moved to a more secure location at Rokeby.

Loudoun County Courthouse

Construction of the first Loudoun County Courthouse began around 1758 and the building was used for over 50 years. The second one was built between 1809-1811 and the cornerstone

Leesburg Inn: Historic postcards, 1900-2008 (VC 0004).
Thomas Balch Library, Leesburg, VA.

for the third (and present) building was laid on April 24, 1894. The courthouse that stands today was constructed on the same site as the courthouse built in 1810-1811.

Leesburg Inn

In 1953 the county purchased the old Leesburg Inn, which had served as a hotel for many years, located adjacent to the courthouse for office space. The Leesburg Inn building housed county offices for about two decades. However, as it fell into disrepair, the county began developing plans for a new county complex, which included razing the old hotel building and replacing it with a new county administration building. The old hotel building was finally demolished in 1974. A new Loudoun County Administration Building, now part of the courts complex, opened on the site of the old hotel in 1976.

McKimmey's Mill: Historic postcards, 1900-2008 (VC 0004).
Thomas Balch Library, Leesburg, VA.

McKimmey's Mill

McKimmey's Mill, now located at Market Station, was named
for a Mr. McKimmey who operated the mill from 1969 until it
became a part of Market Station. The mill, originally located
closer to the W&OD trail, replaced an earlier mill that was
destroyed by fire in 1898.

Mighty Midget Kitchen.

The mill had been operated as a grain mill for over 50 years by the Saffer family, as a feed store by Mr. McKimmey, and is now the Tuscarora Mill Restaurant.

Mighty Midget

Although its name is not one that requires a background story, the Mighty Midget itself is enough of a Leesburg landmark to necessitate inclusion in this effort. The Lilliputian kitchen, measuring only 6 by 9 feet, has been a fixture in the town since 1947. Of particular interest is the fact that it is constructed from the remnants on a World War II bomber.

It originally was located on Route 7 and served take-out food. Its location near Dodona Manor prompted the Marshall's to erect a fence on their property to keep picnickers from destroying their lawn.

However, in 1993, in the name of development along Route 7, it was forced to close. It was ultimately purchased by the Town of Leesburg, moved to its present location, and leased, for twenty years, to Gordon MacDowel, a kitchen-remodeling contractor who subsequently subleased it to Chef Brian DeVaux for a barbeque place and then along with additional space to Nicole Marschall and Timo Winkel for their Döner Bistro.

Old Leesburg Presbyterian Church

Leesburg's oldest extant church, the Old Leesburg Presbyterian Church, located across the street from the Thomas Balch Library was dedicated on May 5, 1804.

Old Stone Church

The earliest known church in Leesburg was the Methodist Church built in 1768 on land deeded by Nicholas Minor on

Old Stone House.

May 11, 1765. After years of use the property was abandoned in 1848 and the building demolished in 1900. The Methodist Historical Society purchased the site in 1961 and visitors can now visit the site and associated cemetery.

Old Stone House

The William Baker House, 106 Loudoun Street was constructed in the 1760s. This stone house is one of the oldest houses in Leesburg.

Osterburg Mill

This mill built in the late 1800s by William Oster in southwestern Pennsylvania was moved to Market Station in 1984. Although from Pennsylvania it is representative of the mills that populated the streams and rivers of Virginia.

Osterburg Mill.

Rust Library

Rust Library is named for William Rust Jr. who also donated 68 acres for Ida Lee Park, which is named for his grandmother.

Thomas Balch Library

Dedicated May 13, 1922 and named for Leesburg-born lawyer who specialized in international arbitration. Balch (1821-1877) had gained fame as the author of the "Alabama Claims" which resulted in a $15 million settlement for the United States from Great Britain after the Civil War.

Tolbert Building

The Tolbert building, originally two dwellings, located on Loudoun Street was moved to its present location at Church and Royal Streets in 1990. It is named for former Vice Mayor John W. Tolbert, Jr., who was the first black person elected to public office in Leesburg (1976).

The Tolbert Building.

Water Tanks

In Leesburg even the town's water tanks and water treatment plant are named.

Carr Tanks—The Carr family is an old Leesburg family and their estate was located near the site of these tanks on Ft. Evans Road. Samuel Carr and John C. Carr were descendants of John Carr born in Ireland, who moved to Loudoun County in 1750, died in 1794, and is buried in Union Cemetery in Leesburg. Samuel Carr is the grandson of Thomas Carr, eldest son of John, and was born in 1814 and died 1881; John Calhoun Carr (1849-1915) was the great grandson of Peter Carr (1740-1812) who was the youngest son of John.

Hogback Mountain Tank—named for nearby Hogback Mountain, part of Catoctin Mountain.

Kenneth B Rollins Water Treatment Plant—A Leesburg Native (1936-1988) and member of the Virginia House of Delegates and a member of state water control board.

A new and existing water tank rise above newly-built commercial space.

Homes

Naming ones House is an old British custom, which began with the gentry naming their manors, halls, and castles. The practice continued with the early settlers in Virginia who gave names to their homes, particularly the larger estates. Actually, in the early years, this custom also served a useful purpose, as addresses were non-existent. Leesburg and the surrounding area are blessed with several notable homes and estates whose names are intriguing.

Belmont

Belmont and Coton Hall in Loudoun and Sully, straddling the Fairfax/Loudoun county line, were Lee family estates. The Belmont estate, located near Ashburn, was started by the Lee family in 1799. Belmont's house was erected 1799-1802 by Ludwell Lee (1760-1836), son of Richard Henry Lee, a signer of the Declaration of Independence. As it sits on the highest point in eastern Loudoun County, it was likely named Belmont after the beautiful hill and view. Belmont is noted for serving as a refuge for President Madison when the British sacked Washington, D.C. during the war of 1812. It was purchased in 1969 by IBM but never used and is now part of the Belmont Country Club.

Dodona

Construction of Dodona Manor started in the 1820s and was completed around the time of the Civil War. Dodona Manor is most noted as the home of General George C. Marshall (1880-1959), author of the Marshall Plan. Marshall lived here between 1941 and 1959 and named it Dodona after the Greek oracle at Dodona, a locale in northwest Greece. Here is a prehistoric oracle site devoted to the mother goddess Gaia. The shrine of Dodona is one of the oldest oracle sites in Greece.

Dodona Manor with statue of Gen. George C. Marshall.

Glenfiddich House

The Glenfiddich House is a completely renovated sixteen-room antebellum home in downtown Leesburg. Besides its connection to Civil War history it is noted for the fact that James Dickey lived here while writing his manuscript *Deliverance*. It was originally called "Harrison Hall" after its builder and first owner, Henry T. Harrison; Glenfiddich, also the name of a well-known Scotch whiskey, is the Celtic word for "valley of the deer."

Holiday Inn at Caradoc Hall

In 1750 William Newton built a log cabin at this locale, which was replaced by his grandson Joseph Newton in 1773 by the building now known as Caradoc Hall. Robert Harper married a daughter of Newton and the Harper family lived here for many years. Harper named the house after Caractacus, a British Chief who opposed the Romans about 50 A.D.

Morven Mansion (at Morven Park).

Hillcrest

Hillcrest, or the Edward Nichols House, was built by Nichols on a knoll (and thus the name) on West Market Street just west of downtown in a rural setting in 1899. Edward Nichols (1847-1923) was a prominent lawyer and businessman. Hillcrest is one of the few homes in Loudoun County that was designed by a registered architect (Lemuel Morris) before 1900.

Morven Mansion (at Morven Park)

This famous home of Westmoreland Davis, Governor of Virginia from 1918-1922, was named by Anice Stockton after fictional Morven, which was home of Fingal, King of the Caledonians, who occupied the west coast of Scotland and is described in the Ossian poem of Temor. Morven Park is on the site of what was known as Swanns Castle, a 19th century plantation belonging to Maryland Governor Thomas Swann, Jr.

Oak Hill

Oak Hill, undoubtedly named for its setting, is noteworthy in that it was designed by Thomas Jefferson and built under direction of James Hogan, designer of the White House and architect of the Capitol. President James Monroe (1758-1831) resided here and this is the locale in which he drafted the Monroe Doctrine. Two Navy ships have been named USS Oak Hill after this estate.

Oatlands

In 1804, George Carter, great grandson of colonial Virginia's renowned Robert "King" Carter, began building his Oatlands estate. Oatlands was a thriving wheat plantation and thus the name. It is now a National Trust Historic Site and a National Historic Landmark.

A young racegoer offers a carrot at Oatlands' annual point-to-point horse race.

Carlheim (Paxton).

Paxton—Carlheim

Paxton is well known to many Leesburg residents; perhaps less so is the home on the grounds. In the early 1870s Charles R. Paxton, a wealthy industrialist from Bloomsburg PA, built a stone mansion here for a summer home. The family named it Carlheim, which is German for Carl's house and alluded to Mr. Paxton's first name. Mrs. Paxton died in 1922, and her will stipulated that the house and 50 acres be established as a home for children in honor of her daughter. The general estate is known as Paxton.

Rock Spring Farm

Rock Spring was a tributary of the Town Spring, which was the primary source of water for the town from 1757-1978.

Big Spring: Historic postcards, 1900-2008 (VC 0004). Thomas Balch Library, Leesburg, VA.

Rockland

Rockland takes its name from the limestone outcroppings found throughout the 600-acre farm. General George Rust built the imposing mansion in 1822, Gen. Rust's son Col. Armistead T. M. Rust, an 1842 West Point graduate who served with the 19th Virginia Infantry during the Civil War, later inherited the property. At his death in 1887, his second wife, Ida Lee, assumed ownership of the estate, including its debts. Rockland is still owned by Rust family descendants.

Rokeby

Rokeby on Gleedsdale Road south of Leesburg was built in 1757 by Charles Binns II. Binns was the Clerk of the Court for Loudoun County and consequently built a brick vault in the basement to store County records. In 1814, during the War of 1812, the Constitution, Declaration of Independence, Articles of Confederation, papers of Washington and all journals of Congress were transported and stored there. In 1820 the then owners named it Rokeby after the poem by Sir Walter Scott as the home and setting described in the poem reminded them of this locale.

Waverly

Located on S. King Street and now comprised of offices Waverly, originally Waverley, was built in 1890 by Baltimore businessman Robert T Hempstone. He named it after the Waverley novels, a long series of popular novels by Sir Walter Scott.

Schools

The word school derives from the Latin word "schola" that basically meant lecture or discussion. The Romans also used "schola" to refer to the learning of singing or a mode of writing.

There are eighteen public and five private schools in the Leesburg area. Once a school is nearing final construction, a committee of parents, teachers, students, and residents is appointed to develop proposed names for the school (naming committee). The school board then votes to decide the official name.

Ball's Bluff Elementary

Named for the October 21, 1812 Civil War Battle of Ball's Bluff, also known as the battle of Leesburg.

Loudoun County High School.

Catoctin Elementary
A very popular name in Leesburg, it derives from the Kittoctons, an American Indian tribe that lived between the Catoctin Mountains and the Potomac River.

Cool Spring Elementary

There was a civil War battle of Cool Spring but it happened in Berryville although troops did travel through Leesburg as they fled from the capital to the Shenandoah Valley.

Douglass School

Douglass school was named for Frederick Douglass, noted black abolitionist and orator. Douglass Community School was the first high school for black students in Loudoun County.

Frances Hazel Reid Elementary

This school was named for "Miss Fannie Reid" who worked for Loudoun Times Mirror for 70 years, ultimately becoming associate publisher.

Heritage High School

Its naming broke the previous tradition of naming high schools with two words prior to "High School."

John W. Tolbert Elementary

John W. Tolbert was a member of city council who championed public education in Leesburg.

J. Lupton Simpson Middle School

J. Lupton Simpson spent almost 40 years as an educator in Loudoun County public schools and was respected by both his students and the community. He died in 1967.

Harper Park Middle School

Named for nearby Harper Park which houses a Stone House built in 1822 by Elias Jenkins as an ordinary (a tavern).

Tuscarora High School

Under construction at the time of this writing, Tuscarora High School is scheduled to open in Fall 2010. A naming committee composed of teachers, students, parents, and members of the community chose the name on September 9, 2008. The Tuscarora (which means "hemp gatherer") were a nearby American Indian tribe. The naming committee also considered the names Leesburg High School and Old George Town High School.

| Streets

The word "street" is ultimately derived from Latin
"via strata" meaning paved road.

A street name or odonym is an identifying name given to a street. The street name usually forms part of the address. The etymology of a street name is sometimes very obvious, but at other times it might be obscure or even forgotten.

In many cases streets are named after numbers, landscapes, or the surname of an important individual. Some streets are named for landmarks that were present along the street when it was constructed. These have often disappeared but the name is retained.

It has also been said that the names of streets in an area provide great insight into the history of the region. This is certainly true in Leesburg. In addition the city's bucolic setting and the area's Civil War heritage are also celebrated in many of the names given to its streets. Although Leesburg is a very peaceful locale there are a lot of names related to war and battle.

Leesburg Street Names

A 1759 map for the town of Leesburg showed four east-west and two north-south streets. The north-south streets were Back and King and those going east west were Royal, Loudoun Market and Cornwall. A 1790 map shows the addition of three more streets; Liberty, North, and Church.

Today, the Town of Leesburg has approximately 1944 street segments, i.e. blocks, with 488 separate streets of unique names. The best part is that in all of these there are no numbered streets, although there is one called First.

General

In 1922 when the first development in the town, Fairview, was established the streets were named for prominent people of the time, e.g., Pershing and Wilson. Themes such as this can be found throughout the town as about 40% (182) of the streets are named for flowers, trees, people and, not surprisingly, the Civil War era. These are shown in Tables 1 through 6.

FIRST NAMES

AMBER	JARED	PATRICE
ANNE	JENIFER	RHONDA
ANTHONY	KENDRA	RICHARD
ARIEL	KENNETH	ROY
BARBARA	KRISTIN	SHANA
BRIAN THOMAS	LESTER	SHERRY ANN
BRIDGETTE	MARYANNE	SHIRLEY
BURT	MAX	TAMMY
CLARK	MAXIMILLIAN	TINA
CLAUDE	MICHAEL PATRICK	TRACY
COLLEEN	MINDY	WILLIAM
EMMET	NATHAN	PATRICE
JACOB	NELSON	

Table 1: First Names

TREES, FLOWERS, AND PLANTS

APPLETREE	GINKGO	SHADETREE
AUTUMN WILLOW	GLADE FERN	SHADY OAKS
BIRCH	GOLDEN LARCH	SILVERBELL
BUNCHFLOWER	GREAT LAUREL	SPARKLEBERRY
BUTTONWOOD	HEARTLEAF	STAR VIOLET
CATTAIL	INDIAN	SWEET CICILY
CEDAR WALK	PAINTBRUSH	SWEET WILLIAM
CEDARGROVE	KALMIA	SYCAMORE HILL
CHERRY	LILAC	TALL OAKS
CLIMBING	ORCHID	TEAROSE
NIGHTSHADE	PEARLBUSH	THISTLE
CLOVE	PERIWINKLE	TROUT LILY
CURRANT	PETUNIA	TULIPTREE
DANDELION	PINK AZALEA	VIRGINIA

FLAMEFLOWER	PRIMROSE	WILDFLOWER
FLOWERING	RED RASPBERRY	WILD ONION
DOGWOOD	REDBUD	WILD TURKEY
GINGER	SARSPIRILLA	WINTERBERRY

Table 2: Trees, Flowers, and Plants

MILITARY / CIVIL WAR

ARTILLERY	FLAG	HOWITZER
BALLS BLUFF	FORT EVANS	JAMES RIFLE
BATTERY	FORT MACLEUD	MUSKET
BATTLEFIELD	FORTRESS	SABER
BEAUREGARD	GARRISON	SENTINEL
BRIGADIER	GENERALS	SHILOH
BUGLE	GUNPOWDER	
CANNON	HAVERSACK	

Table 3: Military / Civil War

LOCATIONS / DESTINATIONS

BALCH SPRINGS	EVERGREEN MILL	MORVEN PARK
CHILDRENS	HAWKS RUN	OAK VIEW
CENTER	IDA LEE	OAKCREST
COCHRAN MILL	KELLYS FORD	MANOR
DEPOT	LEESBURG	OAKLAWN
DODONA	LINDEN HILL	PLAZA
DRY HOLLOW	LOCUST KNOLL	POTOMAC
DRY MILL	LOUDOUN	STATION
EDWARDS FERRY	MARKET	

Table 4: Locations / Destinations

HUNT COUNTRY

BRIDLE CREST	FOXRIDGE	RIDING TRAIL
BROWN ROAN	FOXTAIL	SADDLEBACK
BROWNS MEADOW	HUNTFIELD	STABLE VIEW
EXMOOR	HUNTMASTER	STALLION
FOXHUNT	PADDOCK	

Table 5: Hunt Country

FAMOUS PEOPLE / NOTED RESIDENTS

ADAMS	HARRY BYRD	MONROE
BALCH	HUME	MOSBY
BUCHANAN	JAMES MONROE	PERSHING
BURNSIDE	JANNEY	REVERE
CATESBY	LAFAYETTE	SHANKS EVANS
CHAUCER	LEE	SHERIDAN
COLONEL	LONGFELLOW	TECUMSEH
GRENATA	MADISON	WASHINGTON
FORBES	MAGRUDER	WIRT
GODFREY	MARSHALL	WYTHE
HANCOCK	MCARTHUR	

Table 6: Famous People / Noted Residents

Some Specific Street Names

Some of the more interesting street names are presented below. It is a little surprising that no street, or other artifact, of the town was named for its founder Nicholas Minor.

Andromeda—is a constellation in the northern sky. It is named after the princess Andromeda in Greek mythology.

Ayr—Ayr (on the River Ayr) is a town and port situated in southwest Scotland. The original plantation house of Ayrshire in Upperville was built in 1821 by land-speculator Bushrod Rust.

Beauregard—named after Ft Beauregard one of the civil war forts in Leesburg.

Binns—named for Charles Binns II, original owner of Rokeby.

Cambria—Cambria is the classical name for Wales.

Casla—named for a village in County Galway, Ireland.

Carnaby—The street derives its name from Karnaby House, located to its east, which was erected in 1683. It is not known why the house was so called.

Catesby—Mark Catesby (1683-1749) was an English naturalist.

Catoctin—Derived from the Kittoctons, an American Indian tribe that lived between the Catoctin Mountains and the Potomac River. One variant of the name for the Catoctin Mountains, according to USGS, is Kittocton Mountain. It has been noted that the name Catoctin means "place of many deer." Another meaning has been stated as being "ancient wooden hill."

Chickasaw—One of the many Indian tribes that frequented the region.

Colonel Grenata—Michael Grenata, fondly known as "The Colonel," was an active and highly regarded participant in local Leesburg issues.

Edwards Ferry—Benjamin Edwards owned land at the confluence of Goose Creek and the Potomac River. In 1790 he started a ferry service, which served the area until 1915. This ferry was one of six ferries that traversed the Potomac between Great falls and Point of Rocks.

Ellerslie—Named for a suburb of the city of Auckland City, New Zealand.

Exmoor—The Exmoor Pony is the oldest and most primitive of the British native ponies.

Fenland—Fenland is a section of Cambridgeshire, England

Fort Evans—Named for Fort Evans, built in 1861 near Edwards Ferry Road.

Gleedsdale—Named for John Gleed, once enslaved at Oatlands, who established Gleedsdale.

Hawling—Hawling is a small village in England.

Hetzel—May be named for Pierre-Jules Hetzel, a French editor and publisher best known for his illustrated publications of Jules Verne's novels.

Itasca—Although sounding like an Indian name, it is actually a made up name. In 1832 when Henry Schoolcraft discovered, and proved, that a Minnesota lake was the source of the

Mississippi River, he named the lake Itasca, a name he made up by combining the Latin words veritas and caput, which mean "truth" and "head."

James Rifle—Named for the 14-pounder James rifle, a Civil War cannon.

King—Named in honor of England's King George II.

Loudoun—As with the county, named for John Campbell, Fourth Earl of Loudoun (1705-1782).

Magruder—John Bankhead Magruder (1807 –1871), a career military officer who served in the Confederate army.

Meherrin—The Meherrin Nation is one of eight state-recognized Nations of Native Americans in North Carolina.

Nansemond—Nansemond refers to a group of people of mixed ancestry, who have been recognized as a Native American tribe by Virginia.

Nottoway—The Cheroenhaka (Nottoway) is an Indian Tribe that made first contact with the English in 1608-09.

Occoquan—Occoquan is derived from a Dogue Indian word meaning "at the end of the water."

Octorora—Named for a Civil War steamer.

Paddington—Paddington is an area of the City of Westminster, in London, England, noted for the railroad station and the origin of Paddington Bear.

Powhatan—An Indian tribe also known as Virginia Algonquians.

Rivanna—The Rivanna River is a tributary of the James River.

River Frays—Frays River is a river in England that is commonly called River Frays.

Rust—Named for William Rust Jr. who gave the town land for Ida Lee Park and the Rust Library.

Shadwell—Named for a district of London, England.

Slack—William Yarnel Slack, a Confederate general killed in the Civil War.

Stratford—Named for a city in England.

Sycolin—An unincorporated community south of Leesburg named for the Sycolin Tribe which was an offshoot of the Tuscarora Indians

Tonquin—A 19th century American merchant ship.

Tuscarora—An Indian tribe that inhabited the region-- Tuscarora means "hemp Gatherer."

Wirt—Named for William Wirt (1772-1834), a noted author, statesman, and Attorney General.

Wythe—Named for George Wythe (1726-1806) who was a lawyer, a judge, a prominent law professor and "Virginia's foremost classical scholar."

| Parks and Subdivisions

Park comes from the Old English word parc meaning an enclosed preserve for beasts of the chase.

A young hiker catches a view of the Potomac River at Ball's Bluff Regional Park.

Parks

All of Leesburg's parks are classified by the town of Leesburg as either town parks, community parks, or neighborhood parks, depending on their size and service area. Town parks are the largest in area, over 50 acres; community parks are generally about 20-49 acres; and neighborhood parks are small, generally between 5 and 9 acres, although mini-parks of less than 5 acres are also included in this category. In total the town lists sixteen parks. In addition, there are some county parks in the area. The origin of the names of some of these parks follows.

Balls Bluff

Ball's Bluff Regional Park is a 223-acre park owned and operated by the Northern Virginia Regional Park Authority. Besides marking the site of a famous Civil War battle, the park is noteworthy as it is home to one of the nation's smallest national cemeteries – with only 54 interments, 53 of which are unidentified. The Town of Leesburg has established an 86-acre Veterans Park adjacent to this large regional park.

Balls Bluff is named after the Ball family, which owned the riverfront farm at the time. They were related to George Washington's mother, Mary Ball Washington.

Catoctin Skate Park

Although lacking the bucolic settings of the other Town parks, this park is designed for in-line skaters, skateboarders, and bikes and is one of the most popular locales for those of a certain age range. It is named for its location on Catoctin Circle.

Freestyling at Catoctin Skate Park.

Edwards Landing

Located near what had probably been the landing of Edwards Ferry, operated by Benjamin Edwards.

Georgetown Park

This small (1/2 acre) park located in the historic district is appropriately named after the original name of Leesburg--Georgetown.

Ida Lee

The jewel of all the town's parks, Ida Lee Park was made possible by the donation of Greenwood Farm to the town by William F. Rust, Jr. and his wife, Margaret Dole Rust. The Rusts requested that the park be named in memory of Ida Lee, Mr. Rust's grandmother. The Rusts also donated 3 acres of land from the original farmland for the Rust Library.

Tennis Statue at Ida Lee Park.

Olde Izaak Walton Park

Originally owned by the Izaak Walton league and now a town park, it is named for the famous fisherman and author of "The Compleat Angler."

Raflo Park

In April 1997, the former South Harrison Street Park located near the Town Branch Creek in Leesburg was renamed Raflo Park in honor of Frank Raflo, former mayor, long-time Leesburg resident and noted historian and politician.

Robinson Park

Robinson Park, which provides a baseball field and an all-purpose field, was named after Kenneth Robinson who served on the Parks and Recreation Advisory Commission from 1986-1993.

Entrance to Robinson Park.

Rotary Park

Not surpringly, this park was named to honor the Rotary Club.

Temple Hall Farm Regional Park (nearby)

Temple Hall, built in 1810, was the home of William Temple Thomson Mason, nephew of George Mason.

Tuscarora Creek Park

Naturally named for the creek, which was named for the Indian tribe whose name translates to "hemp gatherers."

Washington & Old Dominion Railroad Regional Park

A Northern Virginia Regional Park Authority park that has become an integral part of the town is known as the W&OD Trail. This regional park is 45 miles long stretching from Alexandria to Purcellville, Virginia. Naturally, it follows the route of the W&OD railroad which was previously known as the Alexandria, Loudoun and Hampshire Railroad and arrived in Leesburg in 1860. The railroad started operation in 1847, passenger service (it was also known as the Virginia Creeper) ceased in 1951, and freight service in 1968. When the W&OD Railroad closed in 1968, its 100-foot wide right of way extended from Alexandria to the center of Purcellville and thus the trail.

A bicyclist enjoys the W&OD Trail.

Subdivisions

In 1922 the first subdivision, Fairview, was developed just west of downtown Leesburg. It seems as though the placement of subdivisions has not ceased since that time. Today there are about 220 subdivisions in the town. Some are named after the developer and others have made up names generally reflecting the actual (or an idealized setting), while some have names that evoke historical strings. We highlight some of these.

Ashburn

Named for nearby Ashburn, which was originally names after a nearby mansion, that name owned by George Lee, great-grandson of Thomas Lee. The section of Farmwell plantation west of Ashburn Road, a 580-acre tract, was purchased in 1841 by lawyer and almost vice-president John Janney, a Quaker, as a summer home. He called the property Ashburn Farm (first known written use is 1870 when he sold the property). It is likely he named the farm after family friends named Ashburn.

Beauregard (Beauregard Heights, Beauregard Estates, Fort Beauregard)

Named for Fort Beauregard, which was a confederate fort during the Civil War.

Belmont

Named for Belmont, a splendid northern Virginia estate started by the Lee family in 1799.

Carnaby Square

Like the street, it derives its name from Karnaby House, located to its east, which was erected in 1683. It is not known why the house was so called.

Exeter Community Center.

Catoctin (Catoctin View)

Catoctin derives from the Kittoctons, an American Indian tribe that lived between the Catoctin mountains and the Potomac River. It has been noted that the name catoctin means "place of many deer." Another meaning has been said to be "ancient wooden hill."

Exeter (Exeter, Exeter Hills, Exeter Square)

Dr. Wilson Cary Selden built Exeter around 1800. Exeter Plantation had a long and storied place in Loudoun County and Virginia history. The home and plantation became established as one of the social centers for the Leesburg area. On October 21, 1861, part of the Battle of Balls Bluff took place on Exeter lands.

The main plantation house burned to the ground in August 1980. A remaining building on the property was later restored and reconstructed as the community center for the Exeter subdivision.

Fort Evans

Named for Fort Evans, a Civil War earthen fort constructed in 1861 to protect Leesburg from possible invasion after Virginia seceded from the Union. The fort was built along Edwards Ferry Road to protect the approaches to the town from the Potomac River. Named for General Nathan George Evans.

Georgetown (Georgetown Mews)

Georgetown was the original name of Leesburg.

Honicon

Derived its name from Leesburg's famed post-World War II contractor, Claude Honicon. He specialized in well-designed stone bungalows.

Paxton

Named for the nearby estate of Charles R. Paxton, a wealthy industrialist from Bloomsburg PA.

Potomac Crossing

Named after the area where General Robert E. Lee turned east to cross the Potomac at White's Ford in 1862.

Tavistock Farms

Tavistock Farms has been an active part of the Leesburg and Loudoun County economy since the early 1800's. The Myers family owned and farmed the property for almost 100 years, from the 1850s until 1950. There are two surviving farm structures on the property: a farmhouse and a springhouse. Tavistock may have originally been named after Tavistock Square in London, England.

Tollhouse (Tollhouse Division)

In the eighteenth century Leesburg had four tollhouses. One has survived.

Trammel

Named after a 1729, 246 acre Trammel Land grant.

Waverly (Waverley Heights, Waverly Park)

Named after the home offices Waverly, originally Waverley, was built in 1890 by Baltimore businessman Robert T. Hempstone. He named it after the Waverley novels, a long series of popular novels by Sir Walter Scott.

Worsley

The McCabe Tavern / Patterson House on Loudoun Street in the historic district has also been known as the Worsley house, after the two sisters that lived there. One of the sisters, Lizzie, was quite active in civic and church affairs.

| Afterword

Having researched and written several books such as this on locations as diverse as the Florida Keys and Pittsburgh, Pennsylvania, it is interesting to note that the names identifying Leesburg's buildings, streets, and parks have developed in a manner that is common to most locales. They evolved through history as the town itself evolved, and for Leesburg reflect the early origins of the 13 colonies, the actions of 250 years of townspeople, and the whims of developers and politicians. And the trend continues as even recent occurrences are now reflected in today's naming process as evidenced by two new features at Ida Lee park, an indoor tennis facility and aquatic center, which were named for A.V. Symington, whose estate donated millions of dollars to fund such new recreational facilities. Undoubtedly the trend will continue as future generations of Leesburgers bestow their influences upon the town and shape tomorrow's names of Leesburg.

One last thought---Even with the bountiful electronic and print resources available today it is almost impossible for one person to adequately address the origin of all Leesburg names. Therefore we have set up an email location:

names@creativeimageryllc.com

for anyone interested in submitting origins of names or suggestions for other entities to be examined. All responses will be appreciated and any that are used in a further edition will be properly credited.

| References

The following provide sources
for more information on historic Leesburg.

Audibert, P. "Leesburg; A Crossroads Town Where the Future Meets the Past." *The Virginia Sportsman*, 2007, pp. 32-38.

Head, J. W. "History and Comprehensive Description of Loudoun County, Virginia." *BiblioLife*, 2009.

Leesburg Planning Commission. *Town of Leesburg Town Plan*. The Town of Leesburg, 1986

Miller, K.A. *Leesburg Historic District: A Survey of the Nicholas Minor Section.* Historic and Architectural Resources, 1998.

Scheel, E. *Loudoun Discovered: Volume 2: Leesburg and the Old Carolina Road.* The Friends of the Thomas Balch Library, 2002.

Smith K.G., Causey E.D., Johnston, E., and K. Laire. *Exploring Leesburg: A Guide to History and Architecture.* The Town of Leesburg.

| Author and Photographer

The Author

Bob Regan is a Research Professor at the University of Pittsburgh. His previous books include *The Steps of Pittsburgh*, *The Bridges of Pittsburgh* and *The Names of Pittsburgh*. He often visits his grandsons and their family in Leesburg.

The Photographer

Jeff Wingard has been passionate about photography since childhood. He began taking pictures with his first SLR, a 35mm Olympus OM-10, at age 11 -- a camera he still uses. An 18-year resident of Leesburg, Jeff now shoots mostly in digital and owns Creative Imagery, LLC.

| Index

Aldie.....................................19

Aldie Turnpike....................11

Alexandria Road....................7

Alogonkian.........................19

Articles of Confederation......15

Ashburn.............................62

Astley....................................

    Margaret Astley.................9

Aubrey's Ferry......................11

Ball's Bluff Elementary..........41

Balls Bluff............19, 56, 57, 63

Battle of Ball's Bluff..............13

Beauregard..........................62

Belmont.......................35, 62

Binns....................................

    Charles Binns II.........40, 50

Campbell...............................

    John Campbell.............6, 52

Caradoc Hall........................36

Carlheim.............................39

Carlyle...................................

    John Carlyle.....................7

Carnaby Square....................62

Carr....................................14

Carr Tanks..........................34

Carter....................................

    George Carter.................38

    Robert Carter.................38

Catoctin........17, 42, 50, 57, 63

Caulkins................................

    Stanley F. Caulkins..........17

Chickasaw...........................51

Civil War.......................10, 11

Claphams Ferry....................11

Conrad's Ferry....................12

Constitution........................15

Constitution House.........15, 26

Courthouse....................26, 27

Davis....................................

    Westmoreland Davis........37

Declaration of Independence. 15

Deliverance....................18, 36

DeVaux..................................

    Brian DeVaux.................30

Dickey...................................

    James Dickey..................18

Difficult Run.........................7

Dodona Manor.........18, 30, 35

Döner Bistro.......................30

Early......................................

    Jubal A. Early.................12

Edwards Ferry.....11, 13, 17, 18, 51, 58, 64

Ellerslie.............................51

Exeter...............................63

    Exeter Hills.....................63

Exeter Square.................63
Exmoor............................51
Fairfax County.....................6
Fairview.....................47, 62
Fenland............................51
Fort Beuregard....................14
Fort Evans...........13, 14, 51, 64
Fort Johnston.....................15
Frances Hazel Reid Elementary
.................................43
George..................................
      King George II.............52
Georgetown..............7, 58, 64
Gleedsdale...............15, 40, 51
Glenfiddich House..........18, 36
Godfrey.................................
      Arthur Godfrey..........17, 18
Godfrey Field.....................17
Goose Creek.................19, 51
Great Road..........................7
Hampshire Railroad.............10
Harper..................................
      Robert Harper.................36
Harper Park..........................43
Harper Park Middle School...43
Harrison.................................
      Henry T. Harrison...........36
Harrison Hall........................36
Hawling............................51
Heritage High School...........43
Hetzel.............................51

Hillcrest...........................37
Hogback Mountain Tank......34
Honicon............................64
Hough...............................
      John Hough.....................7
Ida Lee Park........................58
Immaculate Conception Church
.................................22
Indian War.........................10
Itasca.........................51, 52
J. Lupton Simpson Middle
School............................43
Jenkins..............................
      Elias Jenkins..................43
John W. Tolbert Elementary. 43
King Street............7, 18, 22, 41
LaRouche............................
      Lyndon LaRouche...........18
Laurel Brigade....................12
Laurel Brigade Inn................22
Lee................................
      Francis Lightfoot Lee........24
      Ida Lee......33, 40, 53, 58, 67
      Ludwell Lee....................35
      Richard Henry Lee..........35
      Robert Lee......................9
      Thomas Lee..........8, 24, 62
Leesburg Academy...............24
Leesburg Inn........................27
Leesburg Turnpike...............11
Lightfoot Restaurant............24

Little River Turnpike...........11

Loudoun...................ii, 6, 52

Loudoun County. .ii, 3, 6–8, 11, 13, 24, 26

Loudoun Street......7, 31, 33, 65

Lucketts.............................19

MacDowel...............................

    Gordon MacDowel..........30

Magruder................................

    John Bankhead Magruder. 52

Market Station.................28, 31

Marschall................................

    Nicole Marschall..............30

Marshall.................................

    George C. Marshall....18, 35

Marshall Plan.......................35

McCabe Tavern....................65

McKimmey's Mill................28

Meherrin.............................52

Mighty Midget....................30

Minor....................................

    Nicholas Minor......7, 30, 50

Morven Mansion..................37

Morven Park........................37

Mosby...................................

    John Mosby.....................18

Nansemond.........................52

Newton..................................

    Joseph Newton...............36

    William Newton.............36

Nichols..................................

Edward Nichols...............37

Nolands Ferry.....................11

Nottoway............................52

Nureyev................................

    Rudolph Nureyev...........18

Oak Hill..............................38

Oatlands.......................38, 51

Occoquan...........................52

Octorora.............................52

Old Leesburg Presbyterian Church............................30

Old Stone Church...............30

Oster....................................

    William Oster................31

Osterburg Mill....................31

Paddington.........................52

Paeonian Springs.................19

Patowmack Company..........12

Patterson House..................65

Paxton.........................39, 64

    Charles R. Paxton..........39

Payne...................................

    Flayl Payne....................11

Payne's Ferry......................11

Pittsburgh....................1, 9, 67

Point of Rocks Turnpike......11

Potomac..............................11

Potomac Crossing...............64

Potomac Ridge Road.............7

Powhatan...........................52

Raflo....................................

Frank Raflo...............24, 59

Raflo Park............................59

Rehau................................14

Reid......................................

Fannie Reid....................43

Rivanna..............................53

Robinson Park......................59

Rock Spring..........................39

Rockland............................40

Rocky Run............................7

Rokeby.........15, 26, 40, 41, 50

Rollins...................................

Kenneth B Rollins...........34

Rust.......................................

Armistead T. M. Rust......40

William Rust Jr..........33, 53

Rust Library.............33, 53, 58

Scott.....................................

Sir Walter Scott..........41, 65

Shadwell.............................53

Shenandoah Road.................7

Simpson................................

J. Lupton Simpson...........43

Slack.....................................

William Yarnel Slack........53

Snickersville Turnpike..........11

Sterling...............................19

Stratford.............................53

Swann...................................

Thomas Swann, Jr............37

Swanns Castle.....................37

Sycolin..........................19, 53

Symington.............................

A.V. Symington..............67

Tavistock Farms...................64

Thomas Balch Library...ii, 8, 10, 30, 33

Tolbert...................................

John W. Tolbert........33, 43

Tolbert Building..................33

Tonquin..............................53

Trammel..............................65

Tuscarora.......19, 30, 43, 53, 60

Tuscarora High School.........43

Tuscarora Mill.....................30

Vestal's Gap Road..................7

Washington............................

George Washington.........15

Washington & Old Dominion Railroad..................10, 60

Waverly.........................41, 65

White.....................................

Elijah V. White..........12, 22

White's ferry........................11

William Baker House...........31

Winkel...................................

Timo Winkel...................30

Wirt.......................................

William Wirt...................53

Worsley...............................65

Wythe....................................

George Wythe...............53

| Photo Gallery

Pictures from around town.

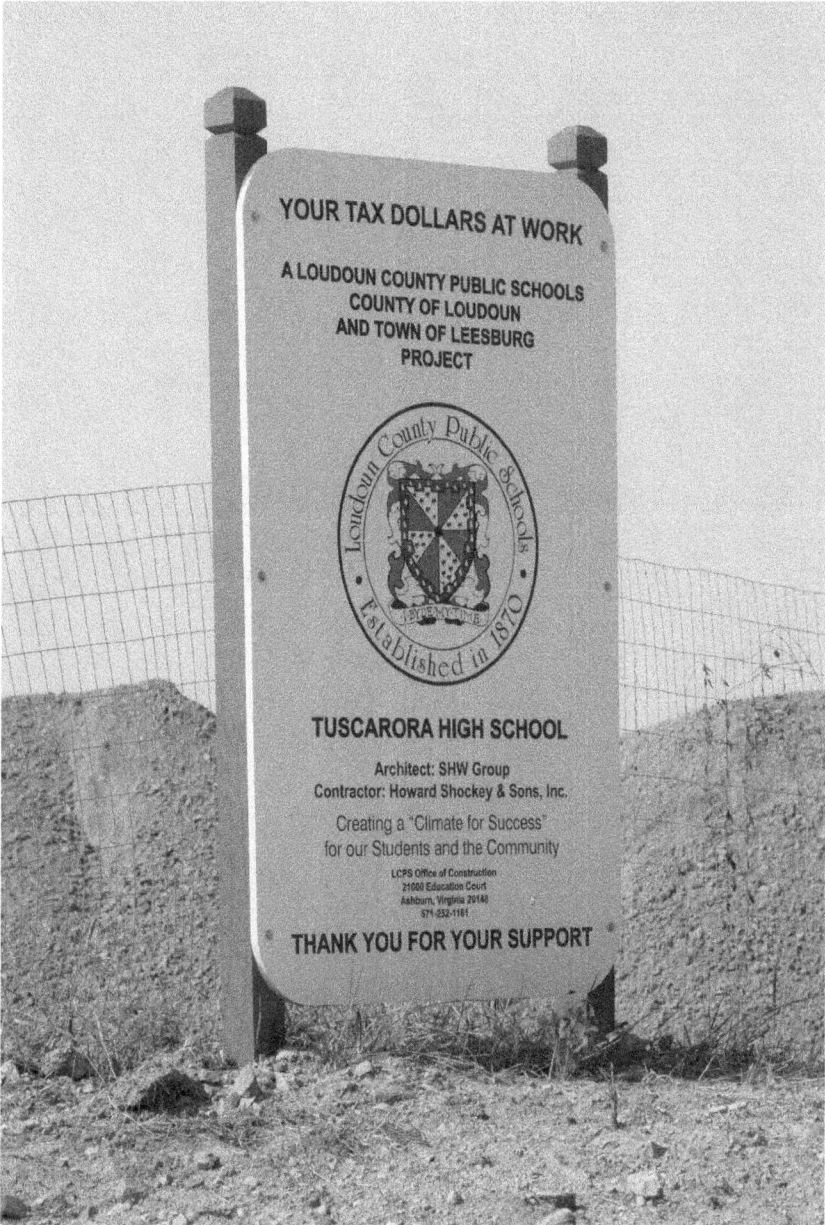

More pictures from in and around Leesburg
can be seen at:

www.creativeimageryllc.com